EVEN SUPERSTARS LOVE THE BENCHWARMER!

"Bob Alexander's cartoons have kept me laughing since I first saw his work in 1974, and 'Benchwarmer's' tops them all!" *—Dave Cowens, Boston Celtics*

"I consider Bob's book a fun reminder to sports fans of events that will long be remembered by participants and fans. Great trivia test!"
—J. C. Snead, P.G.A. Golfer

"'Benchwarmer' is just great!"
—Whitey Ford, N.Y. Yankee Hall of Famer

"Bob's book 'Benchwarmer' is the funniest sports trivia book I've ever seen; a must for any sports fan!"
—Carroll Dale, former G.B. Packer star receiver

"Bob Alexander is a most gifted sports cartoonist. He captures the feel, the drama, and subtleties of sports that a true fan appreciates."
—Curt Gowdy, NBC Sports

HEY SPORTS FANS!

Welcome to the first collection of BENCHWARMER'S SPORTS TRIVIA! The Benchwarmer hopes you will like the cartoons and trivia questions in this book. But Benchwarmer needs your help for Book Two. If you have any sports questions, send them to the Benchwarmer! Maybe your question will be included in the next edition of SPORTS TRIVIA. The Benchwarmer's address is:

BENCHWARMER'S SPORTS TRIVIA
c/o Tempo Books
360 Park Avenue South
New York, N.Y. 10010

Until Benchwarmer's next book...don't take a called third strike!

BENCHWARMER'S SPORTS TRIVIA

By Bob Alexander

tempo books

GROSSET & DUNLAP
A FILMWAYS COMPANY
Publishers • New York

TO JASON,
Middle Linebacker
Green Bay Packers,
1999

ISBN: 0-448-14661-4
A Tempo Books Original
Tempo Books is registered in the U.S. Patent Office
Published simultaneously in Canada
Printed in the United States of America

WHO'LL EVER FORGET "**REG-GEE**" IN THE 1977 WORLD SERIES. BUT CAN YOU LIST THE FOUR INDIVIDUAL RECORDS REGGIE JACKSON SET FOR WORLD SERIES PLAY?

ANSWER: 1.) MOST HOME RUNS IN A SERIES....5.
2.) MOST HOME RUNS, CONSECUTIVE OFFICIAL AT-BATS....4.
3.) MOST RUNS SCORED....10.
4.) MOST TOTAL BASES....25.

WHO HOLDS RECORD FOR PASSING (N.F.L.) EFFICIENCY IN A SINGLE GAME? WHAT IS HIS NICKNAME?

ANSWER:

OAKLAND RAIDER Q.B. KEN "SNAKE" STABLER COMPLETED 25 OF 29 PASSES (86.2%) AGAINST BALTIMORE COLTS ON OCT. 28, 1973.

WHAT PLAYER HOLDS THE RECORD FOR MOST ASSISTS IN A SINGLE N.B.A. GAME?

ANSWER:

BOSTON CELTIC ALL-PRO GUARD BOB COUSY WITH 28 ASSISTS IN A GAME IN 1959.

WHO WON THE FIRST INDY 500?

ANSWER: RAY HARROUN AT 74.59 M.P.H.

JOHNNY UNITAS HOLDS THE RECORD FOR THROWING AT LEAST ONE TOUCHDOWN PASS IN HOW MANY CONSECUTIVE GAMES? WHO WAS THE COLT'S GREAT END WHO CAUGHT MANY OF THESE?

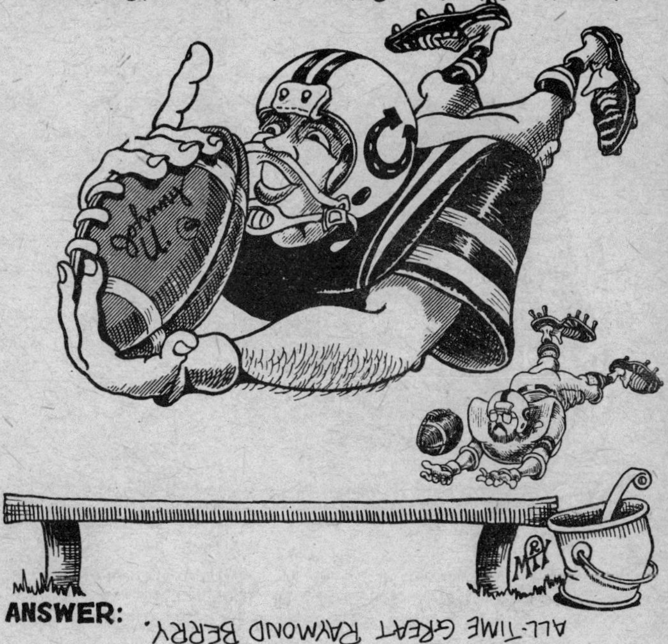

ANSWER:

THE RECORD IS 47 GAMES... MANY CAUGHT BY ALL-TIME GREAT RAYMOND BERRY.

WHEN WAS THE ROOKIE OF THE YEAR AWARD FIRST MADE IN MAJOR LEAGUE BASEBALL.... AND WHO WON IT THE FIRST YEAR?

ANSWER: FIRST AWARDED IN 1947—TO ONE ROOKIE IN THE MAJORS—FIRST WINNER WAS JACKIE ROBINSON - BROOKLYN DODGERS.

DURING BOBBY ORR'S GREAT CAREER WITH THE BOSTON BRUINS, DID THEY EVER WIN THE STANLEY CUP?

ANSWER: YES... IN 1970 AND 1972.

WHAT TEAMS PLAYED BEFORE THE LARGEST CROWD TO WATCH AN INDOOR BASKETBALL GAME? WHERE AND WHEN DID IT TAKE PLACE?

ANSWER:

ON JAN. 20, 1968, A CROWD OF 52,693 PACKED THE HOUSTON ASTRODOME TO WATCH U.C.L.A. PLAY THE UNIV. OF HOUSTON.

WHO WAS THE FIRST TO PLAY IN BOTH A LITTLE LEAGUE WORLD SERIES AND A MAJOR-LEAGUE WORLD SERIES.

ANSWER:

"BOOG" POWELL - LAKELAND, FLA. LITTLE LEAGUE AND IN THE MAJORS WITH BALTIMORE ORIOLES IN 1966 SERIES.

WHAT'S THE SHORTEST PASS ON RECORD FOR AN N.F.L. TOUCHDOWN? WHO THREW IT?

ANSWER:

QB EDDIE LEBARON THREW A 2 INCH TOUCH-DOWN PASS IN WASHINGTON-DALLAS GAME ON OCT. 9, 1960.

WHO INVENTED BASKETBALL... AND WHEN?

ANSWER:

DR. JAMES NAISMITH IN 1891.

NAME HOME COUNTRIES OF TENNIS STARS BJORN BORG, MANUEL ORANTES, AND JOHN ALEXANDER.

ANSWER:

BORG - SWEDEN; ORANTES - SPAIN; ALEXANDER - AUSTRALIA.

WHO BROKE O.J. SIMPSON'S SINGLE-GAME N.F.L. RUSHING RECORD OF 273 YARDS, AND AGAINST WHAT TEAM?

ANSWER:

ON NOV. 20, 1977 THE CHICAGO BEAR'S GREAT RUNNING BACK WALTER PAYTON RAN FOR 275 YARDS AGAINST THE MINNESOTA VIKINGS.

WHO WAS FIRST AMERICAN BASEBALL STAR TO PLAY IN JAPAN AND WHAT NICKNAME DID HE GET BECAUSE OF HIS LACK OF FIELDING ABILITY AT FIRSTBASE?

ANSWER:

HOME RUN SLUGGER DICK STUART, KNOWN AS "DR. STRANGE GLOVE" AND "STONEFINGERS".

WHO HOLDS THE RECORD FOR THE LONGEST SKI JUMP AND HOW FAR?

ANSWER:

ON MARCH 9, 1973 E. GERMANY'S HEINZ WOSIPIWO JUMPED 554½ FEET.

WHAT DO THE FIVE RINGS OF THE OLYMPIC SYMBOL STAND FOR?

ANSWER:

THE RINGS STAND FOR THE FIVE CONTINENTS OF THE WORLD.

WHO WAS ONLY MAN TO HIT HOMERUN OFF SANDY KOUFAX AND CATCH A TOUCHDOWN PASS FROM Y.A. TITTLE?

ANSWER:

ALVIN DARK CAUGHT T.D. PASS WHILE AT L.S.U., LATER AS STAR N.Y. GIANT SHORTSTOP HIT HOMERUN.

WILT CHAMBERLAIN ONCE SCORED 100 POINTS IN AN NBA GAME FOR PHILADELPHIA.... WHEN, WHERE, AND AGAINST WHAT TEAM?

ANSWER:

MARCH 2, 1962, IN HERSEY, PA., AGAINST THE NEW YORK KNICKS.

WHERE DID BOWLING BEGIN, AND WHEN?

ANSWER:

BOWLING'S ORIGIN HAS BEEN TRACED BACK TO 5200 B.C. IN EGYPT.

WHO BEAT OUT CHICAGO'S BOBBY HULL FOR NATIONAL HOCKEY LEAGUE ROOKIE-OF-THE-YEAR, AND WHAT YEAR.

ANSWER:

FRANK MAHOVLICH DID IT IN 1957-58 SEASON.

WHAT TWO COLLEGE FOOTBALL TEAMS PLAYED IN THE FIRST SUGAR BOWL? THE SCORE? THE YEAR?

ANSWER:

TULANE UNIV. BEAT TEMPLE 20-14 IN 1935.

WHAT MAJOR LEAGUE MANAGER IS KNOWN AS "CAPTAIN HOOK" AND WHY?

ANSWER:

CINCINNATI REDS MANAGER "SPARKEY" ANDERSON - BECAUSE OF HOW QUICKLY HE REMOVES A PITCHER FROM A GAME.

WHAT HORSE WON WITH THE FASTEST TIME IN KENTUCKY DERBY HISTORY?

ANSWER:

IN 1973 SECRETARIAT WON THE DERBY IN 1 MINUTE 59 2/5 SECONDS.

WHAT COLLEGE BASKETBALL PLAYER HOLDS THE N.C.A.A. SINGLE GAME SCORING RECORD?

ANSWER:

IN 1954 FURMAN'S FRANK SELVY SCORED 100 POINTS IN A GAME.

WHAT WAS N.Y. GIANT PITCHER SAL MAGLIE'S NICKNAME AND HOW DID HE COME BY IT?

ANSWER:

MAGLIE GOT THE NICKNAME "THE BARBER" FOR THROWING FASTBALLS VERY CLOSE TO THE CHINS OF OPPOSING BATTERS.

WHAT IS THE NUMBER ONE SPECTATOR SPORT IN THE WORLD?

ANSWER:

IT'S NOT FOOTBALL, NOT BASEBALL OR HOCKEY, IT'S SOCCER.

WHAT SPORT IS ASSOCIATED WITH THE TERMS "GLASS JAW" AND "HAYMAKER"? WHAT DO THESE TERMS MEAN?

ANSWER:

THEY ARE BOXING TERMS. "GLASS JAW" MEANS A BOXER WHO CAN EASILY BE KNOCKED OUT WITH A BLOW TO THE CHIN. "HAYMAKER"—A KNOCK OUT PUNCH.

WHAT N.F.L. BACKFIELD DUO WERE KNOWN AS "BUTCH CASSIDY AND THE SUNDANCE KID"? WHAT TEAM DID THEY PLAY FOR?

ANSWER:

THE MIAMI DOLPHIN BACKFIELD OF LARRY CSONKA (SUNDANCE) AND JIM KIICK (BUTCH CASSIDY).

WHO WAS THE FIRST AMERICAN WOMAN TO WIN 3 GOLD MEDALS IN TRACK AND FIELD AT ONE OLYMPICS?

ANSWER:

SHE WAS WILMA RUDOLPH AT THE 1960 OLYMPICS IN ROME.

WHAT FAMOUS SPORTS PERSONALITY WAS THE N.Y. YANKEE RIGHT FIELDER THE YEAR BEFORE BABE RUTH ARRIVED?

ANSWER:

NONE OTHER THAN FOOTBALL GREAT GEORGE "PAPA BEAR" HALAS, WHO PLAYED ONE YEAR, 1919, AND BATTED .091 FOR THE YEAR.

WHAT WAS LARRY O'BRIEN'S JOB BEFORE HE BECAME THE COMMISSIONER OF THE NATIONAL BASKETBALL ASSOC. IN 1975?

ANSWER: HE WAS NATIONAL CHAIRMAN FOR THE DEMOCRATIC PARTY.

WHAT GOLFER RECORDED THE LONGEST PUTT IN A MAJOR TOURNAMENT?

ANSWER: CARY MIDDLECOFF IN 1955 MASTERS SANK AN 86 FT. PUTT.

THE TAMPA BAY BUCCANEERS, A NEW N.F.L. EXPANSION TEAM IN 1976, LOST THEIR FIRST 26 GAMES! WHAT TEAM DID THEY BEAT FOR THEIR VERY FIRST VICTORY? WHAT WAS THE SCORE?

ANSWER:

THE "BUCKS" WON THEIR VERY FIRST FOOTBALL GAME EVER BY BEATING THE SAINTS 33-14 IN NEW ORLEANS ON DEC. 11, 1977.

WHAT RUSSIAN FENCER WAS DISQUALIFIED AND EXPELLED FROM THE 1976 OLYMPICS FOR WIRING HIS ÉPEÉ?

ANSWER:

THE U.S.S.R. FENCER CAUGHT WITH AN ELECTRONIC CHEATIN' DEVICE WAS BORIS ONISHCHENKO. BORIS IS PROBABLY NOW SWORD FIGHTING THE SNOWS OF SIBERIA.

WHITEY FORD OF THE YANKEES HOLDS THE RECORD FOR MOST CONSECUTIVE SCORELESS INNINGS PITCHED IN WORLD SERIES PLAY WITH $33\frac{2}{3}$..... WHOSE RECORD DID HE BREAK?

ANSWER: BABE RUTH...WHO HELD THE RECORD WITH 29 INNINGS SINCE 1918.

WHO IS THE "KING OF SOCCER" AND WHAT IS HIS NICKNAME AND N.A.S.L. TEAM?

ANSWER:

EDSON ARANTES DO NASCIMENTO IS UNDISPUTED "KING OF SOCCER". NICKNAMED 'PELE', PLAYED FOR THE N.Y. COSMOS 1975-77.

WHAT DOES **N.A.S.C.A.R.** STAND FOR, WHEN WAS IT FOUNDED, AND WHO WAS ITS FOUNDER?

ANSWER:

THE NATIONAL ASSOCIATION FOR STOCK CAR AUTO RACING- WAS FOUNDED IN 1947 BY BILL FRANCE, SR.

WHO WAS THE FIRST PLAYER DRAFTED BY THE N.B.A. IN 1975?

ANSWER:

ALL-AMERICAN DAVID THOMPSON OF N.C. STATE ... BUT HE SIGNED WITH DENVER OF THE A.B.A.

WHO WAS **QB.** FOR COACH LOMBARDI'S GREAT PACKER TEAMS..... AND NAME HIS COLLEGE ?

ANSWER:

QUARTERBACK WAS BART STARR, NOW THE HEAD COACH AT GREEN BAY. STARR'S COLLEGE WAS THE UNIV. OF ALABAMA.

HOW DID YANKEE GREAT LOU GEHRIG GET THE NICKNAME "IRON MAN"?

ANSWER:

FOR APPEARING IN A RECORD 2130 CONSECUTIVE GAMES.

WHO WAS FIRST GYMNAST TO SCORE A PERFECT 10.0 IN OLYMPIC COMPETITION? HOW MANY PERFECT SCORES DID SHE GET?

ANSWER:

14 YR. OLD NADIA COMANECI OF ROMANIA. SHE HAD SEVEN PERFECT 10.0's AT THE 1976 GAMES.

WHEN DID JOE LOUIS FIRST WIN THE HEAVYWEIGHT CROWN, WHEN DID HE RETIRE AND WHAT WAS HIS NICKNAME?

ANSWER:

LOUIS, KNOWN AS THE "BROWN BOMBER", FIRST WON THE TITLE ON JUNE 22, 1937 AGAINST JIM BRADDOCK. HE RETIRED MARCH 1, 1949.

WHAT WOMAN WON THE MOST U.S. AMATEUR TITLES?
MIX

ANSWER: GLENNA COLLETT VARE WON 6 TITLES BETWEEN 1922 AND 1935.

MIAMI DOLPHIN QB. DON STROCK LED THE NATION IN TOTAL OFFENSE HIS SENIOR YEAR IN COLLEGE. NAME HIS COLLEGE AND THE YEAR.

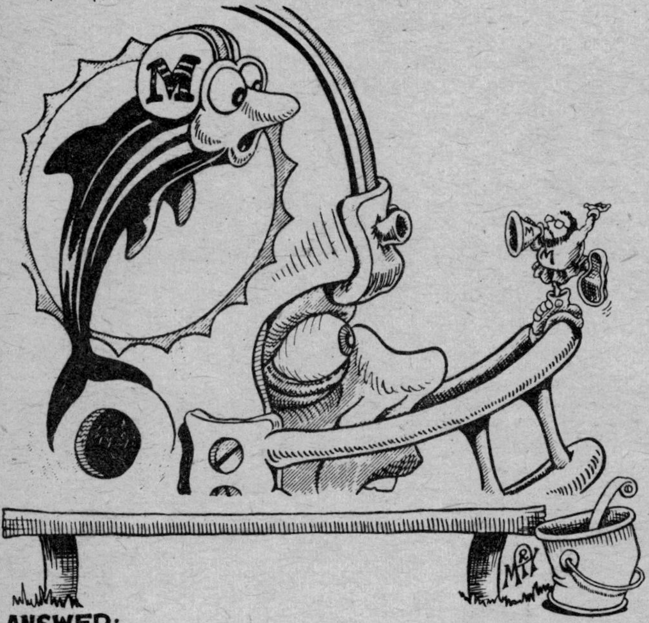

ANSWER:

STROCK LED THE NATION WITH 3170 YARDS IN 1972 AT VIRGINIA TECH.

SECRETARIAT WON THE TRIPLE CROWN IN 1973, BUT BY HOW MUCH DID HE BEAT THE FIELD AT BELMONT?

ANSWER:

SECRETARIAT WON BY 31 LENGTHS.

WHAT IS A "**HAT TRICK**" IN HOCKEY?

ANSWER:

WHEN ONE PLAYER SCORES THREE GOALS IN A GAME.

WHO HOLDS SERIES RECORD FOR MOST STRIKEOUTS IN A SINGLE GAME?

ANSWER: 1968-BOB GIBSON OF THE CARDINALS STRUCK OUT 17 TIGERS

BOBBY RIGGS IS BEST KNOWN FOR HIS MATCH WITH BILLIE JEAN KING. DID HE EVER WIN A TENNIS CHAMPIONSHIP? IF SO, WHAT AND WHEN?

ANSWER:

YES, RIGGS WAS 1939 WIMBLEDON SINGLES CHAMPION.

WHAT IS THE SPORT OF EXPLORING CAVES CALLED?

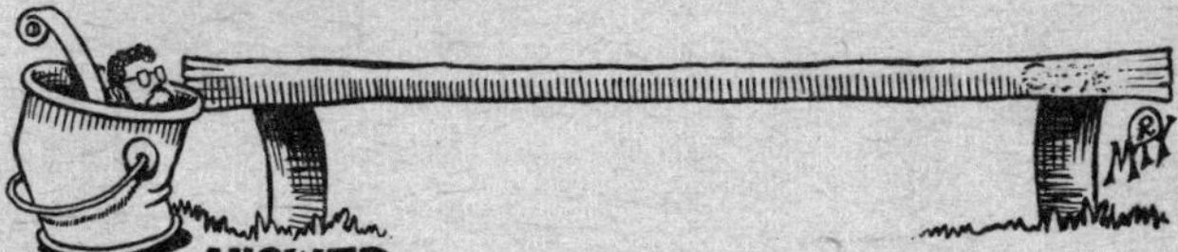

ANSWER: SPELUNKING.

KAREEM ABDUL-JABBAR WAS N.B.A. MOST VALUABLE PLAYER ALL BUT ONE YEAR FROM 1970-74. WHAT WAS THE ONE YEAR HE DID NOT WIN AND WHO WON IT?

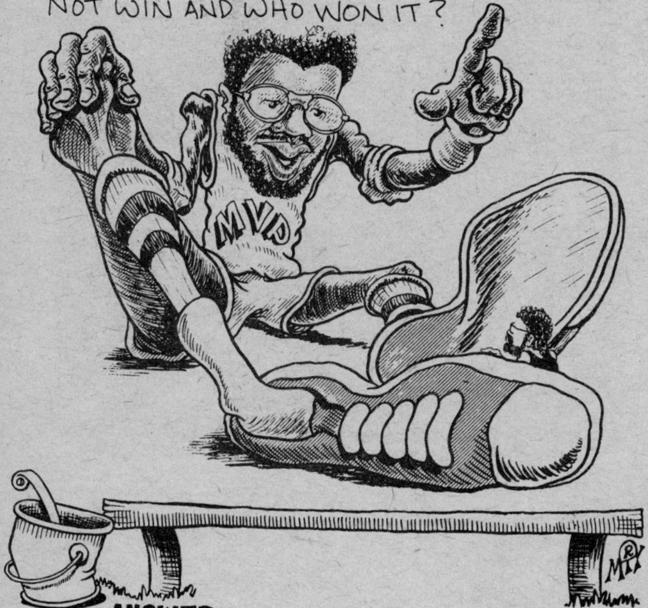

ANSWER:

IN 1973 DAVE COWENS, BOSTON CELTIC CENTER WON THE M.V.P.

WHAT IS FORMER N.F.L. QB. SONNY JURGENSEN'S CHRISTIAN NAME? WHAT PRO TEAMS AND COLLEGE DID HE PLAY FOR?

ANSWER:

SONNY'S CHRISTIAN NAME IS CHRISTIAN. HE PLAYED COLLEGE BALL AT DUKE UNIV. AND PRO BALL FOR PHILADELPHIA AND WASHINGTON.

WHAT IS A "GRAND SLAM" IN TENNIS ?

ANSWER:

WINNING THE SINGLES CHAMPIONSHIP AT WIMBLEDON AND FOREST HILLS. IN THE SAME YEAR, ALSO THE FRENCH AND AUSTRALIAN TITLE; TO HOLD ALL FOUR TITLES.

WHO HAS RAISED THE GREATEST AMOUNT OF WEIGHT EVER, HOW MUCH?

ANSWER:

GEORGIA STRONG MAN PAUL ANDERSON LIFTED 6,270 POUNDS IN A BACKLIFT.

WHO WON THE GOLD MEDAL IN THE MEN'S DOWN-HILL SKIING AT THE 1976 OLYMPICS?

ANSWER:

AUSTRIA'S FRANZ KLAMMER

WHAT WAS THE MOST ONESIDED SCORE IN COLLEGE FOOTBALL HISTORY? WHO COACHED THE WINNING TEAM?

ANSWER:

IN 1916 GEORGIA TECH BEAT CUMBERLAND COLLEGE 222-0. TECH'S COACH WAS JOHN HEISMAN FOR WHOM THE TROPHY IS NAMED.

WHO WAS THE FIRST AMERICAN TO BREAK THE FOUR-MINUTE-MILE RUN?

ANSWER:

JIM RYUN RAN A 3 MIN. 51.3 sec. MILE IN 1966.

THE 1977 AMERICAN LEAGUE CY YOUNG AWARD WINNER WAS YANKEE RELIEF PITCHER "SPARKY" LYLE, BECOMING ONLY THE SECOND RELIEF PITCHER TO WIN THE AWARD. WHO WAS THE OTHER, AND WHAT TEAM DID HE PITCH FOR?

ANSWER:

IN 1974 RELIEF PITCHER MIKE MARSHALL OF THE L.A. DODGERS WON THE CY YOUNG AWARD.

WHO HAD THE LONGEST CAREER AS A COLLEGE FOOTBALL COACH?

ANSWER:

AMOS ALONZO STAGG–57 YEARS, FROM 1890 TO 1946.

WHAT N.B.A. PLAYER SCORED THE MOST POINTS IN A SINGLE PLAYOFF GAME? HOW MANY POINTS AND AGAINST WHAT TEAM?

ANSWER: ON APRIL 14, 1962 THE LAKERS' ELGIN BAYLOR SCORED 61 POINTS AGAINST THE BOSTON CELTICS.

HOCKEY GREAT GORDIE HOWE PLAYED FOR THE N.H.L.'s DETROIT RED WINGS FOR 25 YEARS, THEN DEFECTED TO THE WORLD HOCKEY ASSOCIATION IN 1973. NAME THE W.H.A. TEAM AND HIS TWO SONS WHO PLAYED FOR SAME TEAM.

ANSWER:

IN 1973 HOWE JOINED HIS SONS MARK AND MARTY ON THE W.H.A.'s HOUSTON AEROS, WHERE, AT 45 YRS. OLD, HE WON MOST VALUABLE PLAYER.

FIVE PLAYERS HAVE HIT TWO GRAND-SLAM HOME RUNS IN ONE GAME.....ALL BUT ONE WERE AMERICAN LEAGUERS. WHO WAS THE LONE N.L. SLUGGER?

ANSWER: TONY CLONINGER, A PITCHER FOR THE ATLANTA BRAVES, IN 1966.

HOW MANY TIMES HAS BILLIE JEAN KING WON THE WOMEN'S SINGLES AT WIMBLEDON?

ANSWER:

KING HAS WON SINGLES TITLE SIX TIMES.

WHEN WAS THE NORTH AMERICAN SOCCER LEAGUE FOUNDED AND WHAT TEAM WON THE FIRST CHAMPIONSHIP?

ANSWER:

THE N.A.S.L. WAS FOUNDED IN 1967. THE OAKLAND CLIPPERS WON FIRST CHAMPIONSHIP.

IN THE FAMOUS "SUDDEN DEATH" N.F.L. CHAMPIONSHIP GAME OF 1958 BETWEEN THE N.Y. GIANTS AND BALTIMORE COLTS, WHO SCORED THE WINNING TOUCHDOWN? HIS NICKNAME? HIS COLLEGE?

ANSWER:

COLT FULLBACK ALAN "THE HORSE" AMECHE SCORED WINNING T.D. HIS COLLEGE WAS THE UNIV. OF WISCONSIN.

WHAT N.B.A. PLAYER MADE THE MOST FREE-THROWS IN ONE QUARTER, WHEN, AGAINST WHAT TEAM?

ANSWER:

ON DEC. 6, 1966 RICK BARRY OF THE S.F. WARRIORS MADE 14 FREE THROWS IN A SINGLE QUARTER AGAINST THE N.Y. KNICKS.

1963 FOOTBALL M.V.P.'s WERE JIM BROWN-N.F.L., COOKIE GILCHRIST-A.F.L. 1963 BASEBALL M.V.P.'s WERE ELSTON HOWARD-A.L., SANDY KOUFAX-N.L. WHAT DID THESE FOUR MEN HAVE IN COMMON?

ANSWER:

THEY ALL WORE NUMBER 32.

WILLIE SHOEMAKER HAS MORE WINS THAN ANY OTHER JOCKEY..... WHOSE RECORD DID HE BREAK AND WHEN?

ANSWER: JOHNNY LONGDEN'S RECORD OF 6,032 WINS—BROKEN SEPT. 7, 1970.

HAS ANYONE BESIDES SANDY KOUFAX EVER THROWN FOUR NO-HIT GAMES IN THE MAJOR LEAGUES?

ANSWER:

THE CALIFORNIA ANGELS' FLAME THROWING RIGHT HANDER NOLAN RYAN HAS PITCHED FOUR NO-HITTERS.

WHO WAS THE FIRST BLACK TO PLAY IN THE MASTERS GOLF TOURNAMENT? WHAT YEAR?

ANSWER:

HE WAS LEE ELDER IN 1975.

WHO WAS THE FIRST U.S.A.C. DRIVER TO WIN IN ONE OF ANDY GRANATELLI'S STP SPECIAL RACE CARS?

ANSWER:

MARIO ANDRETTI WAS THE FIRST IN 1969.

IN 1912 JIM THORPE AND THE CARLISLE INDIAN SCHOOL BEAT WEST POINT'S FOOTBALL TEAM 27-6. WHO WAS ARMY'S PUNTER IN THAT GAME?

ANSWER:

THE PUNTER WAS ARMY HALFBACK DWIGHT DAVID EISENHOWER.

AFTER LOU GEHRIG IN THE 1930'S, WHO WAS THE NEXT NEW YORK YANKEE CAPTAIN?

ANSWER: THE YANKEES DID NOT HAVE ANOTHER TEAM CAPTAIN UNTIL CATCHER THURMAN MUNSON IN THE 1970'S.

WHAT WAS THE NICKNAME OF U.C.L.A.'s GREAT BASKETBALL COACH JOHN WOODEN AND WHERE DID HE PLAY HIS COLLEGE BALL?

ANSWER:

WOODEN WAS KNOWN AS "THE WIZARD OF WESTWOOD", PLAYED HIS BASKETBALL AS A GUARD FOR PURDUE UNIV.

WHEN AND WHERE WAS THE FIRST STANLEY CUP HOCKEY CHAMPIONSHIP FIRST PLAYED?

ANSWER:

IN MONTREAL, CANADA IN 1893.

WHAT TEAM DID BABE RUTH HIT HIS FIRST MAJOR LEAGUE HOME RUN AGAINST AND WHO WAS THE PITCHER ?

ANSWER:

RUTH, PLAYING FOR BOSTON RED SOX, HIT HIS FIRST MAJOR LEAGUE HOME RUN ON MAY 6, 1915 AGAINST THE N.Y. YANKEES. YANKEE PITCHER WAS JACK WARHOP.

"THE FINEST FOOTBALL PLAYER I EVER COACHED"
VINCE LOMBARDI

WHAT HALL OF FAME G.B. PACKER WAS LOMBARDI TALKING ABOUT?

ANSWER:

ALL-PRO OFFENSIVE TACKLE FORREST GREGG.

WHO WAS THE FIRST AMERICAN TO WIN THE BRITISH LADIES GOLF CHAMPIONSHIP? WHAT YEAR?

ANSWER:

IN 1947, "BABE" DIDRIKSON ZAHARIAS WON IT.

WHAT WAS THE ONLY WORLD CHAMPION PACER NEVER TO HAVE LOST A RACE?

ANSWER:

THE LEGENDARY DAN PATCH, PROBABLY MOST POPULAR PACER EVER. DAN PATCH DIED ON JULY 11, 1916.

ON AUGUST 19, 1951 A MIDGET, ONLY 43 INCHES TALL, PINCH HIT AGAINST THE DETROIT TIGERS.....
WHAT WAS HIS NAME AND WHO DID HE PLAY FOR?

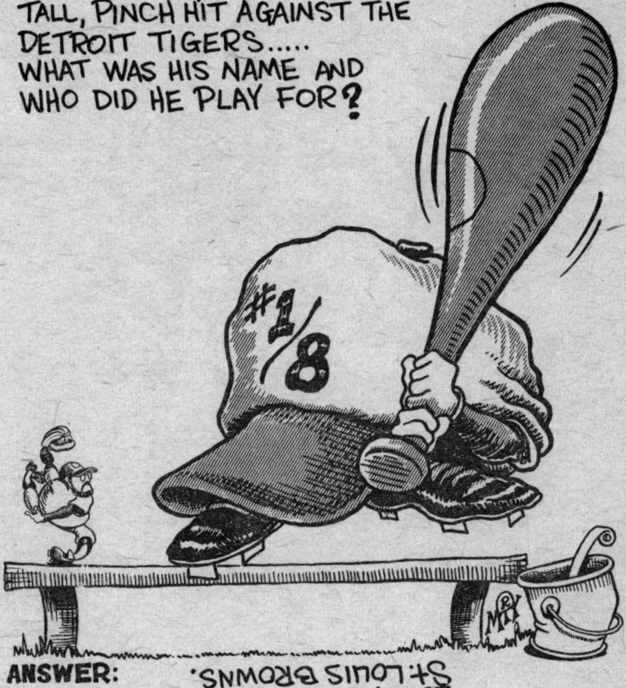

ANSWER: EDWARD GAEDEL OF THE OLD St. LOUIS BROWNS.

WHAT GOALIE HAS GONE THE MOST CONSECUTIVE GAMES WITHOUT A DEFEAT?

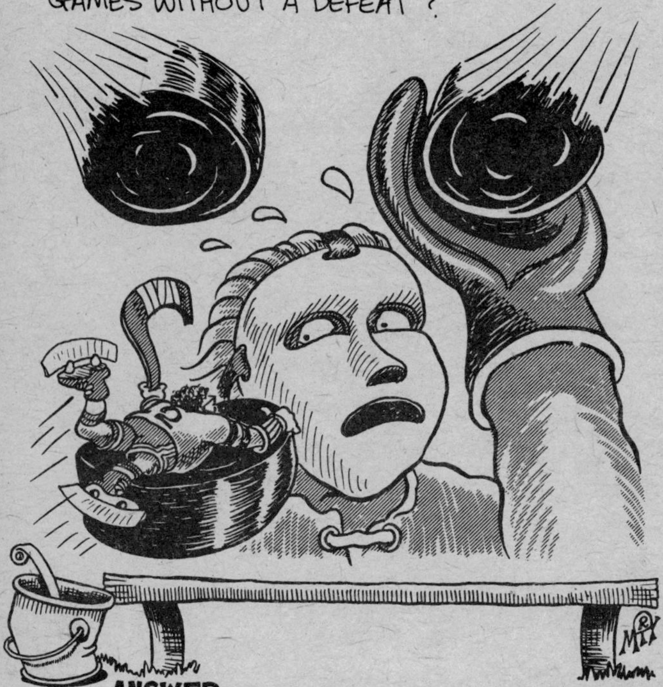

ANSWER:

THE BOSTON BRUINS' GOALIE GERRY CHEEVERS WENT 33 GAMES WITHOUT DEFEAT IN 1971-72.

WHAT G.B. PACKER END CAUGHT 4 PASSES FOR 59 YARDS IN SUPER BOWL I ? WHAT WAS HIS NUMBER AND COLLEGE?

ANSWER:

ALL-PRO END CARROLL DALE, NUMBER 84 WAS ALL-AMERICAN AT VIRGINIA TECH IN 1959-60 YEAR.

WHO WON THE OLYMPIC GOLD MEDAL IN THE DISCUS EVENT FOUR TIMES?

ANSWER: AL OERTER OF THE U.S.A. WON GOLD IN 1956, '60, '64, AND '68 GAMES.

WHAT LEGENDARY RUNNER ALWAYS RAN HOLDING A STOPWATCH? IN HIS 1920-1931 CAREER HOW MANY WORLD RECORDS DID HE SET?

ANSWER:

"THE FLYING FIN" PAAVO NURMI AND IN HIS RUNNING CAREER SET 22 WORLD RECORDS.

HAS THERE EVER BEEN A LEFTHANDED CATCHER IN THE MAJORS?

ANSWER:

YES, FOUR OF THEM. THE ONLY MODERN DAY LEFTY WAS CHICAGO CUB DALE LONG IN 1958.

WHAT AWARD IS GIVEN EACH YEAR TO COLLEGE FOOTBALL'S OUTSTANDING LINEMAN? WHEN WAS IT FIRST AWARDED?

ANSWER:

THE OUTLAND TROPHY, FIRST AWARDED IN 1946.

NAME THE ONLY 300 POUND JOCKEY TO RIDE THE WINNING HORSE AT THE KENTUCKY DERBY.

ANSWER:

SORRY, THERE'S NO SUCH ANIMAL...
...NOT EVEN "BENCHWARMER".

WHAT WOMAN RUNNER WON 4 GOLD MEDALS AT THE 1948 OLYMPICS?

ANSWER:

SHE WAS FANNY BLANKERS-KOEN OF THE NETHERLANDS.

THE FIRST PRO FOOTBALL GAME WAS PLAYED ON AUG. 31, 1895 BETWEEN LATROBE, PA. AND JEANNETTE, PA. .... HOW MUCH MONEY DID EACH PLAYER EARN?

ANSWER: EACH PLAYER RECEIVED $10.

WHAT N.B.A. PLAYER IS NICKNAMED "PISTOL", WHAT WAS HIS COLLEGE ?

ANSWER:

"PISTOL" PETE MARAVICH PLAYED HIS COLLEGE BALL UNDER THE COACHING OF HIS FATHER PRES AT L.S.U.

WHAT BOXER WON THE OLYMPIC GOLD FOR HEAVY-WEIGHTS IN 1972 AND 1976, WHO DID HE DEFEAT IN THE FINALS IN 1972, AND WHAT WAS HIS COUNTRY?

ANSWER:

TEOFILO STEVENSON OF CUBA. IN THE '72 FINALS HE DEFEATED DWAIN BOBICK OF THE U.S.A. HE IS #1 ATHLETIC HERO IN CUBA.

THE RUNNERUP TO TOMMY AARON IN THE 1973 MASTERS GOLF TOURNAMENT ALSO HIT THE LONGEST HOME RUN EVER HIT AGAINST "BENCHWARMER" WHEN BOTH PLAYED HIGH SCHOOL BALL. NAME THE P.G.A. TOUR GOLFER AND HIS HIGH SCHOOL.

ANSWER:

THIS GOLFER DESTROYED MY DREAM OF PITCHING FOR THE YANKEES WITH ONE SWING OF THE BAT. THE P.G.A. TOUR GOLFER IS J.C. SNEAD, WHO HIT THAT HOME RUN AT VALLEY H.S., HOT SPRINGS, VA. IN 1960.

WHAT COLLEGE PLAYER HOLDS THE RECORD FOR BEST CAREER SCORING AVERAGE? WHAT SCHOOL DID HE PLAY HIS BASKETBALL FOR AND WHEN?

ANSWER:

THE ALL-AMERICAN "PISTOL".....
LOUISIANA STATE'S PETE MARAVICH, WITH CAREER AVG. OF 44.2 FROM 1968-70.

ON JAN. 2, 1978 TEXAS MET NOTRE DAME IN THE COTTON BOWL. CAN YOU NAME THE HEISMAN TROPHY RUNNING BACK FOR THE U. OF TEXAS LONGHORNS, AND THE TWO ALL-AMERICAN ENDS FOR NOTRE DAME?

ANSWER:

RUNNING BACK EARL CAMPBELL FOR THE TEXAS LONGHORNS; TIGHT END KEN MACAFEE AND DEFENSIVE END ROSS BROWNER FOR THE "FIGHTING IRISH".

HAS BOWLING GREAT DON CARTER EVER BOWLED A PERFECT GAME?

ANSWER:

CARTER IS CREDITED WITH 13 PERFECT GAMES OF 300.

WHEN AND WHERE DID MUHAMMAD ALI FIRST WIN THE HEAVYWEIGHT BOXING TITLE? WHO DID HE BEAT?

ANSWER:

ON FEB. 24, 1964 ALI DEFEATED SONNY LISTON AT MIAMI BEACH.

WHAT TEAM DOES JAPANESE HOME RUN KING SADAHARU OH PLAY ON ?

ANSWER:

SADAHARU OH PLAYS FOR THE YOMIURI GIANTS.

WHAT IS ANOTHER POPULAR NAME FOR "FREESTYLE" SKIING?

ANSWER:

IT'S POPULAR NAME IS "HOT DOG" SKIING.

HOW MANY TOUCHDOWNS DID CHICAGO BEAR GREAT GALE SAYERS SCORE HIS ROOKIE YEAR?

ANSWER:

SAYERS SCORED 22, A RECORD.

WHAT BASKETBALL PLAYER WAS PAID THE MOST TO SIGN A PRO CONTRACT? WHAT WAS HIS COLLEGE AND HOW LARGE WAS THE BONUS?

ANSWER:

IN 1974 MOSES MALONE OF PETERSBURG, VA. SIGNED RIGHT OUT OF HIGH SCHOOL FOR $3 MILLION BONUS.

WHO WAS DEBART HUBBARD?

ANSWER:

HE WAS THE FIRST BLACK TO WIN A GOLD MEDAL FOR THE U.S.A., WINNING THE LONG JUMP AT THE OLYMPIC GAMES IN 1924 AT THE PARIS GAMES.

WHO WAS THE FIRST RUNNER TO BREAK THE FOUR MINUTE MILE?

ANSWER:

ROGER BANNISTER, 3.59.4 IN 1954.

WHO WAS THE YOUNGEST PLAYER TO HIT 50 HOME RUNS IN A SEASON ?

ANSWER:

AT 24, WILLIE MAYS WAS WHEN HE HIT
51 HOMERS IN 1955.

WHEN WAS THE FIRST ORANGE BOWL GAME? WHAT TEAMS PLAYED?

ANSWER:

THE FIRST WAS 1933, MIAMI OF FLA. BEAT MANHATTAN 7-0.

KYLE ROTE, JR. WAS N.A.S.L. ROOKIE OF THE YEAR IN WHAT YEAR? WHAT SOCCER TEAM DID HE PLAY FOR?

ANSWER:

ROTE WON IT IN 1973 PLAYING FOR THE DALLAS TORNADO.

NAME THE HORSE THAT WAS "HARNESS HORSE OF THE YEAR" THREE YEARS IN A ROW? WHAT YEARS?

ANSWER:

TWO HORSES HAVE DONE IT. BRET HANOVER IN 1964-66; NEVELE PRIDE IN 1967-69.

WHO WON THE SINGLES CROWN AT WIMBLEDON IN 1975, WHO DID HE BEAT?

ANSWER:

ARTHUR ASHE BEAT THE FAVORED JIMMY CONNERS.

WHO HAS WON THE MOST OLYMPIC GOLD MEDALS ?

ANSWER:

MARK SPITZ, U.S.A., WON 9. 2 AT MEXICO 1968, 7 AT MUNICH 1972.

WHAT NATIONAL HOCKEY LEAGUE PLAYER IS KNOWN AS "THE HAMMER"?

ANSWER: DAVE SCHULTZ.

WHO WAS BASEBALL'S LAST TRIPLE CROWN WINNER.... AND WHAT YEAR?

ANSWER:

CARL YASTRZEMSKI-BOSTON RED SOX (A.L.)
WON IT IN 1967.

SOME SAY HE WAS GREATEST ATHLETE OF ALL TIME, HE WON OLYMPIC GOLD AT THE 1912 GAMES. WHO WAS HE?

ANSWER:

THE LEGENDARY CARLISLE INDIAN JIM THORPE WHO HAD THOSE 1912 MEDALS TAKEN AWAY FROM HIM FOR HAVING PLAYED BALL FOR PAY EARLIER.

DID BOBBY OR AL UNSER EVER WIN THE **U.S. AUTO CLUB** CHAMPIONSHIP? WHICH UNSER WON IT AND WHAT YEAR?

ANSWER:

BOTH UNSERS HAVE. AL IN 1970, BOBBY TWICE, IN 1968 AND 1974.

WHO HAD THE HIGHEST FREE-THROW PERCENTAGE FOR A SEASON IN THE N.B.A., WHAT YEAR?

ANSWER:

IN 1959 BOSTON CELTIC BILL SHARMAN HAD A .932 AVERAGE FROM THE FREE-THROW LINE.

JOE NAMATH SIGNED WITH THE N.Y. JETS FOR A $400,000 BONUS. HOW LARGE WAS THE BONUS OF ALL-TIME GREAT JOHNNY UNITAS OF THE BALTIMORE COLTS?

ANSWER:

UNITAS ONLY COST THE COLTS ONE LONG DISTANCE PHONE CALL.

WHO WAS THE YOUNGEST MAN TO WIN THE OLYMPIC DECATHLON?

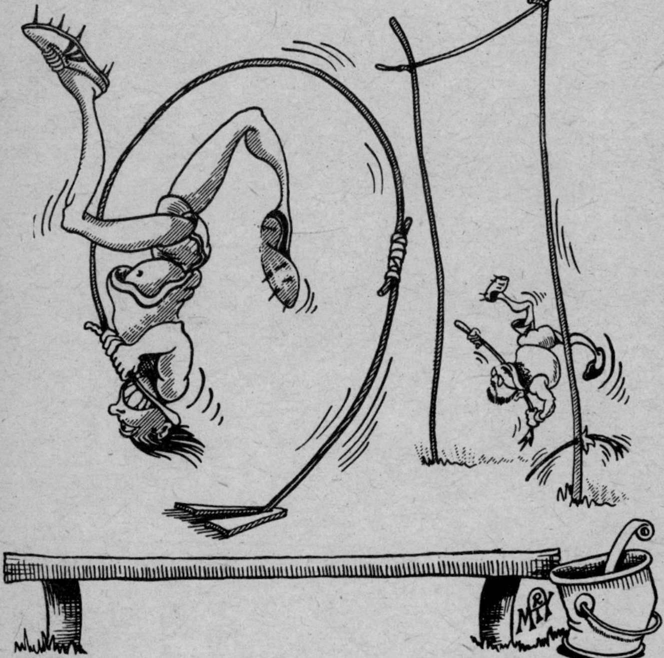

ANSWER: BOB MATHIAS OF THE U.S.A. WON IT AT THE 1948 GAMES WHEN HE WAS ONLY 17.

WHO WAS THE GREATEST "TRICK SHOT" ARTIST OF ALL TIME WITH A RIFLE?

ANSWER:

ANNIE OAKLEY - SHE COULD SHOOT 100 OUT OF 100 IN TRAP-SHOOTING FOR 35 YEARS.

WHAT SCHOOL HAS WON MORE N.C.A.A. BASKETBALL CHAMPIONSHIPS THAN ANY OTHER?

ANSWER:

THE U.C.L.A. BRUINS HAVE WON 10, ALL UNDER COACH JOHN WOODEN.

WHAT YEAR WAS HOCKEY FIRST PLAYED IN THE OLYMPICS ?

ANSWER: THE 1920 GAMES AT ANTWERP.

IN THE FIRST TEN YEARS (1967-76) THAT THE HERMANN TROPHY WAS AWARDED TO THE OUTSTANDING COLLEGE SOCCER PLAYER, WHAT SCHOOL WON IT FIVE TIMES.

ANSWER:

THE OUTSTANDING COLLEGE PLAYER CAME FROM ST. LOUIS UNIVERSITY FIVE OF THE FIRST TEN YEARS.

HOW MANY TIMES DID BABE RUTH HIT FOUR HOME RUNS IN ONE GAME DURING HIS MAJOR LEAGUE CAREER ?

ANSWER:

RUTH, WHO HIT 714 CAREER HOMERS, NEVER HIT FOUR IN A SINGLE GAME.

WHO WAS THE WINNING COACH IN SUPER BOWL ONE?

ANSWER: COACH VINCE LOMBARDI - G.B. PACKERS

JOCKEY GREAT EDDIE ARCARO RODE TWO "TRIPLE CROWN" WINNERS. NAME THE HORSES AND THE YEARS?

ANSWER:

ARCARO WON ON WHIRLAWAY IN 1941 AND ON CITATION IN 1948.

WHO WAS THE FIRST WOMAN TO SWIM THE ENGLISH CHANNEL?

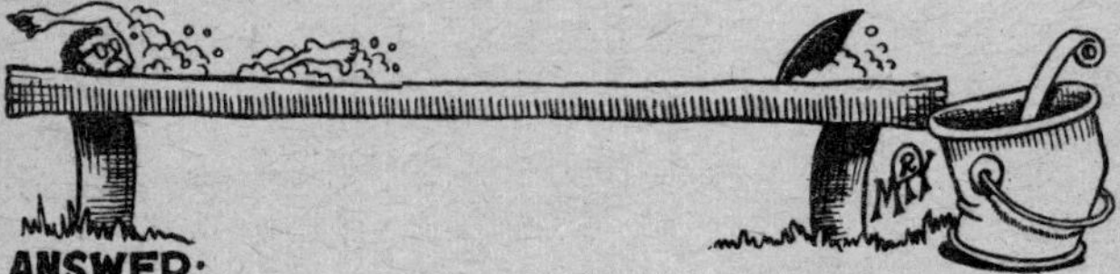

ANSWER:

GERTRUDE "TRUDY" EDERLE IN 1926.

WHO HOLDS THE RECORD FOR THE MOST FUMBLES IN A NATIONAL FOOTBALL LEAGUE CAREER?

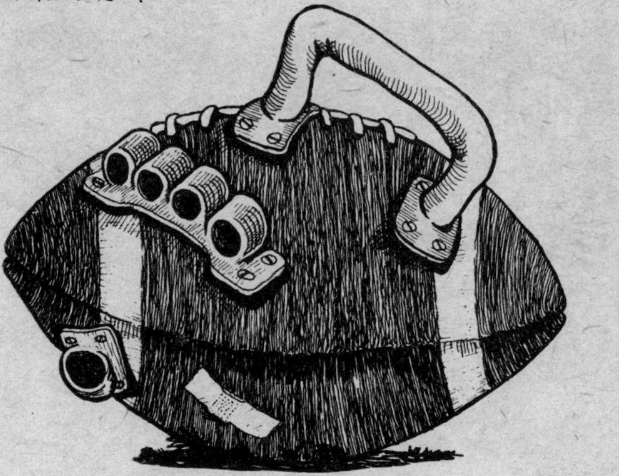

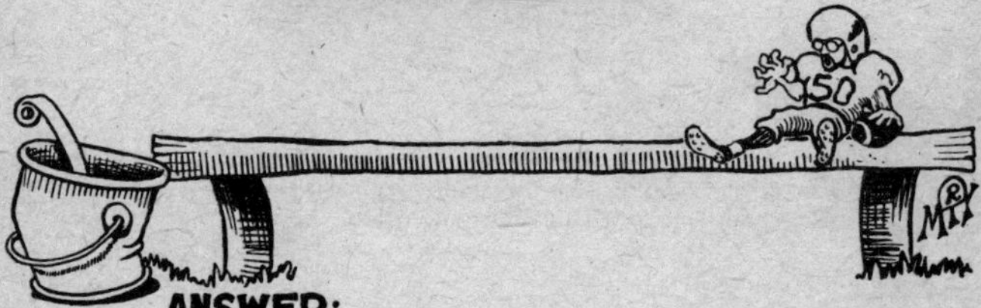

ANSWER:

IT WAS JOHNNY UNITAS WITH 95 FUMBLES FROM 1956-1972.

WHO BROKE DETROIT'S TY COBB'S ALL-TIME BASE STEALING RECORD, AND WHEN?

ANSWER:

ST. LOUIS CARDINAL LOU BROCK BROKE COBB'S 50 YR. OLD RECORD IN 1977 SEASON.